Greater Than a Tou
Wadi Rum
Jordan

50 Travel Tips from a Local

>TOURIST

Um A'yube

Copyright © 2017 CZYK Publishing

All Rights Reserved. No part of this publication may be reproduced, including scanning and photocopying, or distributed in any form or by any means, electronic or mechanical, or stored in a database or retrieval system without prior written permission from the publisher.

Disclaimer: The publisher has put forth an effort in preparing and arranging this book. The information provided herein by the author is provided "as is". Use this information at your own risk. The publisher is not a licensed doctor. Consult your doctor before engaging in any medical activities. The publisher and author disclaim any liabilities for any loss of profit or commercial or personal damages resulting from the information contained in this book.

Order Information: To order this title please email lbrenenc@gmail.com or visit GreaterThanATourist.com. A bulk discount can be provided.

Lock Haven, PA

All rights reserved.

ISBN: 9781521451380

\>TOURIST

>TOURIST – Wadi Rum, Jordan – Um A'yube

DEDICATION

This book is dedicated to the wonderful place I call home, Wadi Rum. To my husband without whom I would never have been able to live here and to my husband's family who have welcomed me into their lives, with tolerance and grace.

>TOURIST – Wadi Rum, Jordan – Um A'yube

BOOK DESCRIPTION

Are you excited about planning your next trip?

Do you want to try something new while traveling?

Would you like some guidance from a local?

If you answered yes to any of these questions, then this book is just for you.

Greater Than a Tourist - Wadi Rum, Jordan by Um A'yube offers the inside scope on Wadi Rum. Most travel books tell you how to travel like a tourist. Although there's nothing wrong with that, as a part of the Greater than a Tourist series this book will give you tips and a bunch of ideas from someone who lives at your next travel destination.

In these pages you'll discover local advice that will help you throughout your stay. Greater than a tourist is a series of travel books written by locals.

Travel like a local. Get the inside scope. Slow down, stay in one place, take your time, get to know the people and the culture of a place. Try some things off the beaten path with guidance. Patronize local business and vendors when you travel. Be willing to try something new and have the travel experience of a lifetime.

By the time you finish this book, you will be excited to travel to your next destination.

CONTENTS

CONTENTS

Author Bio

How To Use This Book

WELCOME TO > TOURIST

Introduction

1. Travel to Wadi Rum – the best ways to get here

2. Orientate yourself

3. Consider volunteering

4. Plan your visit in advance

5. Try Bivouac camping

6. Learn some Bedouin Arabic

7. Syncronise your visit with a waxing, waning or new moon

8. Walk up Um Ad Dami (with a Bedouin guide)

9. Drink some Bedouin tea

10. Nap in the middle of the day in Summer

11. Listen to the Azan (call to prayer) from the Nabatean Temple

12. Pack essential items for camping and hiking

13. Try some Bedouin Games

14. Scramble up to the Burdah Arch (with a Bedouin guide)

>TOURIST – Wadi Rum, Jordan – Um A'yube

15. Bring the kids

16. Taste traditional Bedouin food - Zaarb

17. Taste traditional Bedouin bread – Arboot

18. Taste traditional Bedouin bread – Shraak

19. Visit the Women's co-operative

20. Hike the Jordan Trail (or at least some of it)

21. Discover Al-Shillelleh spring

22. See how many different Keffiyah styles you can spot

23. Clear up some mis-conceptions about the weather

24. Experience a hot air balloon ride

25. Roll down a red sand dune

26. Entering Jordan through the Eilat/ Aqaba – Wadi Araba border?

27. Read the inside scoop on Khazali Canyon

28. Purchase the children's e-book "Bedouin Bedtime", also by Um A'yube

29. Ride a camel through the desert

30. Wake up for sunrise

31. Scramble up one of the many small mountains to watch the sunset

32. Visit the "heart" of Wadi Rum

33. Watch Bedouin coffee being prepared and have a taste

34. Spend at least one day at your Bedouin camp in the desert, with

no activities planned

35. Taste some fresh dates (khalal or rutab)

36. Play with some Bedouin children

37. Visit a secret winding sand dune "canyon"

38. Prepare some riddles and jokes to tell around the fire

39. Listen to Bedouin music – Bedouin singing and Oud playing

40. Visit during a full moon

41. Take a walk around Rum village

42. Follow tracks in the sand

43. Count shooting stars

44. Try to spot a desert hedgehog

45. Don't forget to look down

46. Take a silly action selfie jumping over a sand dune

47. Watch your Bedouin guide change a flat tyre

48. Learn about Bedouin herb/ plant use

49. See how many different types of rock you can count

50. Disconnect yourself from the world (just keep your camera with you)

> TOURIST

> TOURIST

> TOURIST

Author Bio

Um A'yube is from a grassy green, grey and rainy town in the South of England. She has a BA in Fine Art and a MA in Residential Landscape Architecture. Living in the desert in Jordan with a Bedouin husband and three children wasn't really in her plan for life, but what life goes as one plans?

Living in the desert has given Um A'yube a new appreciation for rain, which she now holds to be one of the most wonderful things in Allah's creation.

Um A'yube spends her time taking care of her three young children, her little house, a handful of goats and geese, and in her spare time writing and illustrating children's stories about Bedouin life of which she self published the first one this year.

Um A'yube has been living in the Wadi Rum desert since 2009. She considers herself very blessed to have the opportunity to live in such a beautiful place with people of such fascinating character. She would like to thank her husband for that!

How To Use This Book

This book was written by someone who has lived in an area for over three months. The author has made the best suggestions based on their own experiences in the area. Please check that these places are still available before traveling to the area. Get ready to enjoy your next trip.

>TOURIST – Wadi Rum, Jordan – Um A'yube

WELCOME TO > TOURIST

Introduction

Wadi Rum is often the place people love the most after their travels in Jordan, yet we only receive about 5% of all the visitors to the country. As knowledge about the area increases this percentage is probably on the rise, but many people do miss out. I urge you to take the time to visit, and to at least spend one day and night in the desert.

Wadi Rum is located in the South of Jordan about a 1 hour drive from Aqaba, and a 2 hour drive from Petra. The whole protected area of desert is 723 KM squared. The valley with the name Wadi Rum, starts a little before the Visitor Center and stretches South to Rum village, then as far as Khazali Canyon. This is the valley I have called my home since 2009, and the valley described by Lawrence of Arabia in his book "The Seven Pillars of Wisdom".

Wadi Rum is a breathtakingly beautiful desert landscape and the wonderful, mischievous, honourable people that live here is what makes the place truly unique. A visit to Wadi Rum is about culture, and landscape. There is a lot of history here but the desert renders societies ineffectual, insignificant, and the archeological evidence of past peoples is not grand like in Petra. If you take a Jeep tour think of it as a journey through this area, without it there is nothing to focus on, no rhythm to the visit. The Jeep tours take you through the landscape and THAT is the site, the places you visit along the way are moments to focus on different features of the desert, to walk around, explore, play, photograph, or an opportunity to reflect on the harsh environment people have survived in for so many years.

In my 50 tips I have tried to include things to help you get the most out of your visit to Wadi Rum, there are ideas for things to do, tips where I draw your attention to details many people miss. Mostly the tips I suggest could be carried out independently by a low budget traveler staying in Rum Village (I have included references to google maps and GPS co-ordinates when relevant), but some of them require a guide, an organised activity and a stay at a Bedouin Camp.

I have not recommended any specific camps because I don't want to be biased, but I do recommend you choose a guide/ camp who is from Rum village. This way you can be sure you are using a local guide.

There are many Bedouin camps and the best way to choose is to consider the area they are placed, if they are near or far to Rum village, the tours they offer, and how they operate. Each traveler will have their own preferences, so research and choose the best place for you. The Bedouin Camps will always have a website and ways to contact them directly (e-mail, phone). These days most camps locations can be seen on google maps.

People on a low budget can also stay at the Rest House – either on the roof or you can pitch your tent there for a low cost. There are some Bedouin guides who will offer low cost accommodation in the village.

Insha'Allah (God willing) you will enjoy the tips I have given, and they will help you get more out of your experience visiting Wadi Rum.

>TOURIST – Wadi Rum, Jordan – Um A'yube

>TOURIST – Wadi Rum, Jordan – Um A'yube

1. Travel to Wadi Rum – the best ways to get here

Travelling to Wadi Rum is not complicated in itself but there are some important facts you can be aware of when planning your journey.

Firstly, if you want to keep your budget low and use buses when possible then you should visit Petra prior to Wadi Rum. There is a daily early morning bus that comes to Wadi Rum from Petra. As long as there are enough tourists the bus will run (even on Fridays). This bus is most reliable during the busy seasons – March, April, May and Sept, Oct, Nov, Dec (last two weeks only). The rate is 7JD p.p. (2017). The bus always stops at the Visitor Center and then continues inside the protected area to Rum Village, the driver dropping people at the houses of the various guides they have booked with. Very convenient really, for a bus!

There is also a bus from Aqaba to Wadi Rum, but the timing of this is less convenient for travellers, and doesn't run on Fridays. The rate is 3JD p.p. (2017). The bus leaves Aqaba at approx 1-1.30pm, arriving in Wadi Rum at 2.30-3pm. The bus leaves from the Aqaba bus station close to a public garden and the souk. The bus station is divided into two parts, a road running between them. The Aqaba-Wadi Rum bus leaves from the section of the bus station on the same side of the road as the Police Station. The bus has Wadi Rum – Aqaba written on it in English.

Many people will rent a car while in Jordan and this is a good option for getting to Wadi Rum, making arrival and departure much simpler. Rental cars can be driven all the way to Rum Village for free, and most guides/ camps have free parking facilities in the village.

GPS co-ordinates for Rum Village are:

Latitude: 29°34'40.79"N

Longitude: 35°25'13.22"E

If you look on **Google maps** enter: Wadi Rum, Jordan. This locates Rum Village. Look at the satellite view.

(You can also enter these digits to google maps and that will show you the start of the village: 29.578011, 35.420274).

2. Orientate yourself

The protected area of Wadi Rum is about 723 KM squared, no one expects you to find your way around 100% by yourself. However, if you orientate yourself a little PRIOR to your visit you will be well placed to avoid some scams and you will be better able to compare and choose from the tours you are being offered by any guides you contact.

There is only ONE village inside the protected area and this is Rum Village. The village is small and where the tarmac road ends. Beyond Rum village to the South, East and West there is a considerable distance before you will see man made innovations like tarmac roads, electricity pylons etc. If you really want to experience the desert as a wilderness then Rum Village is where you should be meeting your guide and starting your tour from. All the guides based in Rum Village are locals.

A key point to be aware of is that the desert doesn't just start and stop along the protected area boundaries. Therefore, it is possible to visit beautiful areas of desert and not be inside the protected area. There is an area to the North of the protected area (close to a village called Diseh/Disi) where tours are carried out by various local and non-local operators. The area is still beautiful but you will see things around like electricity pylons, a working train track, more tarmac roads and larger villages. There are not building regulations for the camps outside the protected area. There are many Bedouin Camps offering accommodation in this area, for the above reasons these camps tend to be larger, more commercial, have more "facilities", and are often used as "party" destinations by young people from Amman. Foreign and Jordanian Tour companies almost 100% use the Diseh camps because they are afraid their guests cannot handle the simpler facilities at the camps inside the protected area (i.e. electricity is not on all night, smaller bathrooms, sometimes mattresses on the floor rather than bed frames and other similar things, in short a camping experience).

Personally, I am an advocate for the simpler camps inside the protected area but I think it is good to have a variety of options so a greater diversity of people are able to visit the area. In the end most people who leave unsatisfied do so because they have not properly researched the area and have either gone to a commercial camp when they would have preferred a quiet one, or have gone to a quiet one when they are out of their comfort zone camping.

There is a map of the protected area on the official website (http://wadirum.jo/) and I would strongly recommend you have a look at it so you can tell if you have entered the protected area or if you are going to Diseh. The map is located on the homepage at the bottom in the "brochure".

The Visitor Center where you buy your entrance ticket to the protected area (5JD p.adult, children under 12 yrs free, as of 2017) is about 7KM on the tarmac road before you reach Rum Village. Make sure you pay for the ticket at the office, or get the Jordan Pass to avoid hassle here (a lot of scams are centered around relieving you of your 5JOD rather than it going to the Visitor Center).

3. Consider volunteering

Slow travel is always a special way to experience a new place. The majority of tourists visit Wadi Rum over one day and night. Volunteering gives you the opportunity to spend much longer in the desert getting to know its ways and the people here. Volunteering helps enable locals to run their businesses better because Westerners have written language and internet skills they don't have yet. These days Bedouin people are educated and fully literate in Arabic. However, while a few can read and write English moderately well or well, the majority will only speak English having learnt orally through their work. Volunteers help them to answer tourist e-mail enquiries professionally, manage social media accounts, and booking platforms etc. There are LOTs of opportunities listed on websites such as: helpx.net, workaway.info and wwoofinternational.org. Placements range from listings by young guides wanting to start up their own business (they are usually looking for help with websites, and other relevant marketing tasks), to established camps/ guides who usually look for admin support running their business and practical help at their camp. Most listings will want a stay of 1 month or more, but some may accept a shorter stay. These opportunities are a great way to really get under the skin of Wadi Rum and a good way to meet women and children, as well as the male guides who you will help. Bedouin Culture is wonderful, nuanced, and anyone who would like to try to get a good insight into Bedouin people should consider volunteering as a possibility.

Warning: This section should be obvious, but just in case I would like to include the information. When deciding to spend a long time in the desert it is wise to first read up a little on Bedouin culture, especially as a solo female traveler. While you will be so much safer in Wadi Rum than in most cities over the world, you should be aware how eye contact and friendliness on your part can be mis-understood on the males part as flirting. Platonic relationships don't exist in Bedouin culture. You should NEVER agree to go on night time walks alone in the desert with any guide, even if you are curious. There are a number of women who have had bad experiences attempting relationships and marriages in the village with local Bedouin. Western and Bedouin cultures are VERY different and adapting to live here is no small task. Any budding relationship should be approached with extreme caution on the part of the westerner, until you are certain you know the young man in question very well (i.e. knowing someone a few days, weeks or months is not enough to know anyone very well). It is very easy to be charming for a short period of time.

Also be aware that Bedouin women will not want you to take pictures of them. This is because they are very much in control of who does and does not see them. A photograph takes on a life of its own and then they can potentially be seen by others who would not normally see them. You should ALWAYS ask before taking photographs of anyone, and you should not post pictures of women on social media without their express permission.

4. Plan your visit in advance

Many places in the world are best visited spontaneously. However, in Wadi Rum some time put aside to do some research prior to your visit will be well worth the effort. There are lots of Camps and guides, all of them a little bit different. Some are close to the village, some are far from the village, some are not even inside the protected area, some have views to the sunset, some are hidden close to the rock formations, some have simple facilities, some are more fancy, some will pack themselves full with 100 people if they get the chance, some keep numbers under 30 people even when very busy, and so on. Considering what you would like to do and how you would like to experience the desert in advance is absolutely the best thing to do here. The camps are all very spread out, and inaccessible unless you have a Jeep, so unlike in a town if you end up at a accommodation you don't like, you don't have much scope to pack your bags and go find another one.

Most guides and camps have websites where you can see pictures of the camp, see the tours they offer, and get an idea of how they run things. They usually have a listing on TripAdvisor where you can read reviews from their past guests.

I strongly recommend doing your research first, and contacting the camps you are interested in yourself first. They will usually have a e-mail contact, and telephone number, some will use WhatsApp. Please don't use booking.com. This website is driving a trend in non-transparency as different camps join and to avoid paying booking.com large fees each month (not easy for Bedouin as access to banking is limited) they put very low fees for the accommodation, and then when people arrive to stay they find there are lots of extra charges they did not anticipate. Or the companies make the tours more expensive to make up for the loss they have sustained by giving such low rates for the accommodation. The standard rates for one night accommodation with dinner and breakfast included is 20-25JD p.p per night. There are some "luxury" options which are priced higher. If you have found somewhere 1/2 or less than 1/2 of the standard rates beware of hidden costs.

5. Try Bivouac camping

Many guides will offer Bivouac camping – or camping "under the stars". If you have never experienced sleeping outside with just the breeze on your face, and the stars twinkling above you, then I cannot recommend it enough. Take your intrepid spirit on a journey Bivouac camping in Wadi Rum and you will not regret the experience. There is something perfectly wonderful about waking up at dawn, not because of the alarm but because you are outside and feel the gradual arrival of light. Then remembering as you open your eyes you are surrounded by the most beautiful desert in the world. Observing the soft reds, pinks, oranges, multitude of browns, yellows, whites, merging into the pastel blues and violet of the sky as the sun arrives, from your comfy bed, is a priceless experience. All this without any mention of the night before, the meal prepared on the fire in front of your eyes, and the vast night sky ever present above you. Do go for proper Bivouac camping (not close to a Camp, unless it is an isolated one). Some camps advertise this option as sleeping in a "cave". The "caves" are rock overhangs close to the given camp where you can sleep outside. A good option if you are nervous, but if you really want to experience the desert to yourself, then choose Bivouac camping and ask to be away from any other nearby permanent camps.

6. Learn some Bedouin Arabic

Bedouin Arabic is a little different to the Arabic spoken in the towns in Jordan. Everyone understands each other, but different words are used. A good way to strike a rapport with your guide, especially if he doesn't speak much English is to make some effort to learn some Bedouin words while you are here. Here are a couple of examples to get you started:

Esht (Eshh-t) – thank you to a male.

Eshti (Eshh-tee) – thank you to a female.

Taheesh (Ta-hee-sh) – the reply to Esht. Much like "you are welcome".

Taheeshi (Ta-hee-shi) – the reply to Eshti. Much like "you are welcome".

You are highly likely to hear somebody say to you at some point:

Ahlan-wa-sahlan (Ah-lan wa sah-lan) – this means "you are welcome".

The reply (very important to say when speaking Arabic) is:

Ahlan Beek (Ah-lan Bee-k) – to a male.

Or Ahlan Beeki (Ah-lan Bee-ki) – to a female.

Gowak (Go-wak) – Hello – to a male.

Gowki (Go-w-ki) – Hello – to a female.

7. Syncronise your visit with a waxing, waning or new moon

One of the highlights of visiting Wadi Rum for many people is the view to the night sky. In the evenings the Milky Way is regularly seen, along with shooting stars. To get the best nighttime sky views visit when the moon is small, ideally on the nights when the new moon is due to arrive.

Summer (Autumn and Spring also to a lesser extent) is the prime time to come for the best nighttime sky views, because the evenings are usually warm and pleasant.

There are lots of websites online that give details of the moon phases so you can check what the moon will be doing when you plan to visit. I often use this website:

https://www.timeanddate.com/moon/phases/

8. Walk up Um Ad Dami (with a Bedouin guide)

Um Ad Dami is the highest mountain in Jordan. While this sounds very dramatic, actually at 1883 meters high the mountain is not a record breaking highest mountain. The walk itself starts at a high altitude already so most of the hard work Is done before you start. Great news for people who want to tick off a "highest mountain" with very little danger or difficulty. Um Ad Dami is perhaps one of the most accessible highest mountains in the world!

The hike itself is about 2-3 hours up and down, the route is steep with rubble and loose rocks so firm boots are better than trainers, but other than that it is not a very challenging hike. Uber fit people have been known to do it in 1.5 hours. People who are not accustomed to hiking can take longer than 3 hours. Most people fall in the average of 2-3 hours. The walk is well worth the effort you do put in, for the spectacular views from the top, which include a glimpse over the border to Saudi Arabia, and views to the North of a deep dry sand river bed winding up the valley. From the top you have a brand new perspective of the desert and its scale, as you see it stretching away from you in all its glory, in every direction for miles, and miles and miles.

9. Drink some Bedouin tea

If you manage to visit Wadi Rum and avoid drinking any Bedouin tea then you will have achieved something exceptional. However, avoiding tea is not what I recommend. Bedouin tea is sweet, strong, and smoky.

The tea is often served with a herbal addition serving to enrich the flavour more. The most popular herbal addition is sage or mint. Thyme is also used (this is favoured in milky tea with goats milk). There are also some wild herbs that sometimes can be found when you are on your trip. If your guide finds these herbs he may then use them in the tea.

Even if you are not a big fan of tea or sugar I would say live on the wild side and try it just once... You will be surprised at how delicious tea can be.

If you are health conscious and reluctant to consume sugar, bear in mind that when a person becomes dehydrated they need to replenish their body with glucose and sodium. In short, sugar and salt. Therefore, it is no surprise that the Bedouin diet is rich in both substances.

10. Nap in the middle of the day in Summer

If you visit Wadi Rum in the summer by far the best thing to do when you are exploring the desert is to rest during the hottest time of day. This way you reduce your chances of getting heat stroke, you adapt to the local pace of life, and sometimes stopping to absorb the environment in a quiet way is an enriching experience, rather than just keeping busy the whole time.

If your guide goes to sleep on your lunch break, take his lead and have a nap too... Or at least lie back on the sand, look up at the rock formations, the sky and enjoy the peace, quiet and some time disconnected from the modern world.

>TOURIST – Wadi Rum, Jordan – Um A'yube

>TOURIST – Wadi Rum, Jordan – Um A'yube

"Yet I wondered fancifully if he had seen more clearly than they did, had sensed the threat which my presence implied – the approaching disintegration of his society and the destruction of 'his beliefs'. Here especially it seemed that the evil that comes with sudden change would far outweigh the good. While I was with the Arabs I wished only to live as they lived and, now that I have left them, I would gladly think that nothing in their lives was altered by my coming. Regretfully, however, I realize that the maps I made helped others, with more material aims, to visit and corrupt a people whose spirit once lit the desert like a flame."
— **Wilfred Thesiger, Arabian Sands**

11. Listen to the Azan (call to prayer) from the Nabatean Temple

The Nabatean Temple is located a short walk from the Rest/ Guest House in Rum Village and can easily be visited independently for no charge. The Rest House is the first building on the right as you reach Rum Village from the Visitor Center. Between the Rest House and the first shop there is a Jeep track "road". Follow the road and up on the hill at the foot of the Jebel Rum cliffs you will find the Nabatean Temple. At this place there is a captivating echo. When the Azan goes it is a wonderful, transporting experience to listen from this spot. Muslims pray five times a day, and the times are determined by the sun. Fajr is at Dawn. Dhur is around midday when the sun is at its highest point in the sky. Asr is in the afternoon when the shadows are about three times the length of the object. Magrib is about 10/15 minutes after the sun sets. Lastly Isha is in the evening at the end of the first third of the night.

Google Maps co-ordinates: 29.577920, 35.415160

GPS: 29°34'40.5"N 35°24'54.6"E

12. Pack essential items for camping and hiking

Visiting Wadi Rum and experiencing the desert at its best really involves at least one day and night. When using the smaller Bedouin camps inside the protected area (recommended) you should pack the following:

A torch/flashlight

A First aid kit

A Sheet sleeping bag – if you aren't comfortable without your own sheets

Covered shoes: firm trainers, or soft hiking boots

Sandals or flip flops to wear in the evening around the camp

In the winter warm clothes are essential including a jacket, jumper, socks, hat, gloves

In Autumn and Spring warm clothes as well as coolers layers are advisable

13. Try some Bedouin Games

Whoever you choose to be your camp and guide in Wadi Rum, for certainty your guides will know a multitude of hilarious and entertaining Bedouin Games. If they don't show you any themselves during the long evenings around the fire, be sure to ask them to show you some Bedouin Games.

There are sand games, clapping games, games like a puzzle that you have to work out, games with stones, and many more.

My favorite is a group clapping game. You go around in a circle one-by-one clapping once, then when a person decides to clap twice the direction changes. If the wrong person then fails to clap or claps when they shouldn't have they are out. This continues until you have a winner. A simple but entertaining game.

14. Scramble up to the Burdah Arch (with a Bedouin guide)

This has to be my favorite natural rock bridge in Wadi Rum. There are four famous natural rock arches here (Little Bridge, Um Frouth Arch, and Disi Kharaz Rock Bridge), along with hundreds of smaller and less famous natural arches dotted around the area. To see the Burdah Arch up close you need to hike and scramble through a labyrinth of yellow sandstone mountain. Along the way you get wonderful views across the valleys around this mountain, and high up on the mountain you find flat areas of sand with plants growing. Ideal mountain habitats for wildlife, protected from Jeep damage and over grazing. The hike is challenging so you should not attempt this without the right experience and certainly not without a guide unless this is the kind of hiking you do regularly. There is a guide book by Tony and Di Howard that includes details of the route up to the Burdah Arch for those people who are experienced hikers/ climbers (Treks and Climbs in Wadi Rum, Jordan).

15. Bring the kids

If you are parents then don't have any doubts about bringing your children along to enjoy the experience. The Wadi Rum desert is like a very large, wonderful playground and from my experience children always love the place, without exception. They love climbing around on the rocks, playing in the sand (you can bring a bucket and spade for the younger ones and they will stay busy for HOURS), the animals, the fire at night, the sweet Bedouin tea and the food which is simple and usually popular with even the fussiest children.

Bedouin people love children and you will find your guide will come up with no end of games that keep them entertained.

Maybe 5 years ago I met a family with two very active, lively and intense little girls. After spending two days and nights here in the desert, their parents told me that this was the first time they had ever been anywhere the girls would play together for more than half an hour without input from their parents. The whole family loved it and their parents got to enjoy sitting back and watching them play for the first time.

Other parents have told me that while staying in Wadi Rum they have seen their teenagers engaged and disconnected from technology for a sustained period of time without complaint for the first time.

16. Taste traditional Bedouin food - Zaarb

Zaarb is a wonderful combination of barbecue and oven roast. Chicken (rubbed with spices, tomato puree, and salt) and vegetables are put on a layered metal frame, while a big fire is made inside a metal barrel under the ground. Once the fire has burnt down leaving only hot embers at the bottom of the barrel, the metal frame is lowered inside. A metal lid is put over the top and buried under sand. The food is left to slow cook for at least 2 hours and the result which, they usually dig up while you watch, is really marvelous. Tender, smoky, juicy, and not to mention, healthy too! The onions are put in whole, so you peel off the skin and then eat the hot, juicy insides. The Zaarb is served at all Bedouin camps with rice, bread and salads. The only reason they might not serve it is if there are not many guests on the given night you are staying. If you want to try it just indicate to them you would like to try it when you book and then they will usually happily provide it for you.

17. Taste traditional Bedouin bread – Arboot

Bedouin people have two kinds of bread which traditionally they would make daily when living as nomads in the desert. The first is called "arboot", pronounced "arr-boo-t". The dough is made with wholemeal flour, water and salt. After the dough is made while it sits, a fire is made and hot embers are produced. Once there is enough embers, a large flat area of hot embers is prepared. The dough is kneaded out into a large thick (about 1 cm) flat oval and placed onto the embers. The dough is then covered with more embers and ash until it cannot be seen. After baking this way the bread is removed and the result is a bit like a crusty healthy naan (Indian bread). Arboot is very filling and would usually have been baked when travelling, or when out grazing with their animals because it is very low tech to make. When inclined they will also break the bread into lots of small pieces, add a sour milk/ yoghurt drink called "sheneena", mush up the mixture, then make a hollow in the center to which they pour olive oil or goat ghee. This mixture is not pretty, but delicious and very, very filling. I like to refer to it as concrete for the stomach. The first time I ate it for lunch I didn't feel hungry again until the next day! You will need to ask for this specially if you would like a chance to try it. Trying arboot should be possible for lunch or if you are Bivouac camping.

18. Taste traditional Bedouin bread – Shraak

The second kind of bread is a much more skilled process to make and also requires special equipment. For this reason mostly women know how to do it, and the craft is passed from mother to daughter. Making shraak is a fading skill but some young women do still know how. Women over 30 yrs all tend to know how. The work is hot and tiring and better done as a team. Usually women will make this bread first thing in the morning. The wholemeal dough is made and then rolled into lots of balls around the size of a pool ball. A hot fire is prepared. Then they have something which looks a bit like a very large upside down wok on legs. This is placed over the fire. Then the women manipulate the dough balls into large flat thin circles much like the South Indian "Dosa". The dough is placed onto the hot metal curved surface to cook briefly and then turned over. The result is something like a smoky very large savoury pancake. Delicious. If you get the opportunity to try it don't hesitate! This bread is not usually served at the Bedouin Camps. You can find it in some of the shops in Rum village in the mornings. The bread is not necessarily kept on display so you should ask if they have any "shraak". Some women have a small business where they sell their handmade shraak to the shops in the village. Otherwise you can also buy this bread from bakeries around Jordan, but these will be machine made, rather than hand-made.

>TOURIST – Wadi Rum, Jordan – Um A'yube

19. Visit the Women's co-operative

There are two co-operatives in Rum village (there is also a glitzy one at the Visitor Center, needless to say I prefer the more grassroots one in the village). You don't need permission to visit them, and most mornings you should find them open. My favorite one is a short walk from the girls' school. If you stand with your back to the girl's school (next to the phone tower on the East side of the village) you will see a road in front of you. Follow this road and on the right hand side about 2-3 houses down you will see the women's co-operative. The building/house looks very unassuming, there is a worn sign outside indicating it's presence. Inside they have various products the local women make – from goat hair rugs, to wall hangings, to necklaces made from Wadi Rum stones, to soap, to bags. You can also see the loom they use to weave the handmade goat hair thread into rugs.

20. Hike the Jordan Trail (or at least some of it)

The Jordan Trail is a wonderful, challenging long distance hiking trail from Um Qais in the North of Jordan, to Aqaba in the South of Jordan. The concept was originally the idea of Tony and Di Howard when they realised the walks they were doing could easily be connected into a long distance trail. Many years later now the trail is ready and officially complete.

The section from Petra to Wadi Rum is very remote and beautiful. The section from Wadi Rum to Aqaba is also really interesting and takes you down the most famous valley of Wadi Rum, then through the harsh mountains to the West of Wadi Rum and down into Aqaba to the sea.

The first guided group thru hike took place this year in 2017 and finished in Aqaba in May. You can read all about it on the blog of Andrew from the National Geographic: http://www.myjordanjourney.com/.

The tour company Experience Jordan is also involved with the trail and regularly organizes weekend trips from Amman to different sections of the trail. http://experiencejordan.com/

You can read all about the trail, see information about the routes on the Jordan Trail Website: http://jordantrail.org/

The hike has some sections which are somewhat developed and some sections where there is no trail at all so you either need a guide or to be in a group, or to be a very experienced wilderness hiker. Hiking alone must be done with a GPS. The Jordan Trail should not be attempted as an unsupported thru hike without proper research, preparation and relevant experience.

>TOURIST – Wadi Rum, Jordan – Um A'yube

"By day the hot sun fermented us; and we were dizzied by the beating wind. At night we were stained by dew, and shamed into pettiness by the innumerable silences of stars."
— **T.E. Lawrence, Seven Pillars of Wisdom: A Triumph**

21. Discover Al-Shillelleh spring

Al Shillelleh Spring is one of the lesser known springs in Wadi Rum. All in all there are about 5 springs from Jebel El Qattar at the South of the Wadi Rum valley to Jebel Rum at the North of the valley, next to Rum Village. There is a base of hard granite rock at the foot of the mountains, then on top sits sandstone. All along the seam between the two rock types you will find springs. The most famous one was recently named " Lawrence Spring" after Lawrence of Arabia who was in the area during the Great Arab Revolt. However, in his book " The Seven Pillars of Wisdom" the spring he describes visiting is actually Al-Shillelleh Spring. Not the one most Jeep tours go to, named: Abu Aineh/ Lawrence Spring.

Al- Shillelleh Spring is easy to find and can be visited without a guide. Start at the Rest House (first building on the right entering the village after the Visitor Center). With your back to the Rest House facing South you will see in the distance, to the right, along the base of the Jebel Rum mountain, a small red building, standing alone. You need to walk across a flat sandy area (with some Bedouin tents and animal pens situated on it) to this building.

Google map co-ordinates for the building: 29.573876, 35.413000

GPS co-ordinates for the building: 29°34'25.9"N 35°24'46.8"E

Once you reach the building you will see a rough path and built stone steps. If you look at the satellite view on google maps and zoom in you can see the imprint of the path on the mountain. Follow the path as it first winds up the mountain side, and then South along the contours of the mountain. Along the way you get nice views down to Rum Village. Also along the way there is a large slab of rock (a bit like a wedge of cheese) with inscriptions on it. Once you reach the Spring it is nice and cool, with plants and herbs growing there. There is a "room" cut into the rock that collects the water and this is where Lawrence of Arabia had a shower. You can also see Nabatean inscriptions at the spring which are also mentioned by Lawrence of Arabia in his book.

Take a walk to discover the spring on hot afternoons as this is the first place to receive shade.

22. *See how many different Keffiyah styles you can spot*

Bedouin men wear a large square folded piece of material on their head when in public. This is called a "*keffiyah*". There are many colours which, don't have any particular significance. Saudi's tend to favour a red and white one, Palestinians the black and white one. However, ultimately there is no significance to the colour and in the end the choice comes down to taste. How you wear the *keffiyah* is another story! The style of how you wrap it around your head, can indicate your mood, where you are from and even other things like if you are on the lookout for a fiancé.

See how your guide wears his and how many different styles you can spot while in Wadi Rum, and Jordan.

Why not ask your guide to show you how to tie one yourself? There are Bedouin tents at Lawrence Spring, Khazali Canyon and the Um Frouth Arch where you can buy your own *Keffiyah* and learn how to tie it over some smoky, sweet Bedouin tea. You can also buy them in Rum Village, Aqaba and other towns in Jordan.

23. Clear up some mis-conceptions about the weather

Many people think the desert is freezing at night, and scorching by day. While this is somewhat true there is a lot of variation in temperature throughout the year. There are seasons and the nights are not freezing all year around, while the days are not scorching all year around.

See the following table:

Month	Temperatures		Possibility of rain?
	Day	Night	
January *	Around 5-15 degrees	Around 0-10 degrees	We usually get rain 2-4 times in the month. Rain brings temperatures to the lower end of the scale and can last from a day to five days. We can get snow on rare occasions.
February *	Around 8-20 degrees	Around 5-10 degrees	We usually get rain 2-3 times in the month. Rain brings temperatures to the lower end of the scale and can last from a day to five days.
$ * March	Around 10-25 degrees	Around 10-15 degrees	We usually get rain 2 times in the month. Rain brings temperatures to the lower end of the scale and can last from a day to five days.
April * $	Around 15-30 degrees	Around 10-20 degrees	We usually get rain 1-2 times in the month. Rain brings temperatures to the lower end of the scale and can last from a day to five days.
May	Around 20-35 degrees	Around 15-25 degrees	We don't usually get any rain in May. If there was some rain, it would be a very small amount for a very short time. Or with humid weather and a thunderstorm.

>TOURIST – Wadi Rum, Jordan – Um A'yube

June	Around 30-40 degrees	Around 20-30 degrees	We don't get rain in June.
July	Around 30-40 degrees	Around 20-30 degrees	We don't get rain in July.
August	Around 20-30 degrees	Around 15-25 degrees	We don't get rain in August.
September * $	Around 15-25 degrees	Around 15-25 degrees	Sometimes we get the first rain of the year this month. Maybe it could rain 1-2 times. Rain brings temperatures to the lower end of the scale and can last from a day to five days.
October * $	Around 15-25 degrees	Around 10-20 degrees	We usually get rain 2 times in the month. Rain brings temperatures to the lower end of the scale and can last from a day to five days.
November *	Around 10-15 degrees	Around 5-15 degrees	We usually get rain 2-3 times in the month. Rain brings temperatures to the lower end of the scale and can last from a day to five days.
December *	Around 5-15 degrees	Around 0-10 degrees	We usually get rain 2-4 times in the month. Rain brings temperatures to the lower end of the scale and can last from a day to five days.

* Can be strong winds

$ My favourite months of the year

24. Experience a hot air balloon ride

The Wadi Rum desert is spectacular. The kaleidoscope of different coloured sands, the massive towering mountains dramatically emerging from the sandy floor, the strange rock formations sculpted by water and wind. However, seeing it from above will give a wonderful overview of the area and memories to last a lifetime.

Some local guides will arrange it for you but I recommend having direct contact with the Balloon Company – The Royal Aero Sports Club of Jordan. Their website which includes a booking form is: http://www.rascj.com/

>TOURIST – Wadi Rum, Jordan – Um A'yube

25. Roll down a red sand dune

Rolling down hills is gloriously silly. Rolling down sand dunes is gloriously sillier. Most Jeep/ 4x4 tours will include a visit to a large Red Sand Dune. The largest is Al-Hasany, a marvellous pile of redder than red sand (also seen in the Transformers 2 film – they weren't in Egypt really), heaped up against a red sandstone gnarly mountain. The climb up is a good workout and running or rolling down is an opportunity to revert to your childhood.

Warning: Rolling down sand dunes causes a ridiculous amount of fine red sand to embed itself into every part of your clothing, shoes and body. You will be picking it out of your ears for days.....

26. Entering Jordan through the Eilat/ Aqaba – Wadi Araba border?

Beware: This border was once the simplest and best border to use when entering Jordan from Israel. However, since January 2016 things have changed.

The border will no longer issue VISAs on demand on arrival. You MUST get the VISA in advance from your home country Jordanian Embassy.

The only way around this is to buy the Jordan Pass online in advance. Then they will issue a free VISA at the border. As long as you then stay 3 or more consecutive nights in Jordan there is no charge when you leave. If you stay less than three nights the charge is 60JD p.p. There are some restricted nationalities and these people cannot use the Jordan Pass to get a VISA, they must get one in advance.

Israeli citizens (any number), restricted nationalities and groups of non restricted nationalities of more than four people have no option but to book their time in Jordan with a Jordanian tour company (they will not allow you to travel independently around). If you haven't done so they will not allow you entry from this border. If you are a group and want to travel independently, use another border...

The Jordan Pass website has a excellent FAQ section which gives information about using the Wadi Araba border to enter Jordan:

https://www.jordanpass.jo/

27. Read the inside scoop on Khazali Canyon

Khazali Canyon is one of the most visited sites in Wadi Rum, and there is a reason for that. The dramatic high cliffs of the mountain, with two shades of sandstone, a red layer topped with a white layer, all offer a striking experience for the eyes. The canyon itself is a crack like fissure and walking inside you are in shade all year around. Inside the canyon you will often find pools of water and during rain large volumes of water rush through the canyon, and down the mountain side producing dramatic waterfalls. The rain giving a live demonstration on how the shapes of the mountain have formed.

My favourite thing about Khazali Canyon is the **hidden features**.

When you enter the canyon examine the walls (both sides) above the "water line" on the rock. There you will see several examples of very old inscriptions including several pairs of feet (how many can you spot.. I have counted three pairs). These are particularly interesting to me as it demonstrates their age. In Bedouin Arab culture the soles of the feet are seen as dirty (you do walk around in you know not what) and pointing the soles of your feet at someone is very rude. This then poses the question were these inscriptions made at a time before this particular aspect of Bedouin culture had developed?

Secondly, as you walk through the canyon you will see perfect circles cut into the rock. The circles are clearly man made and must be modern because they are perfectly round indicating they were machine cut. These holes were actually cut by the film crew when they were filming

"Lawrence of Arabia" here. The holes were cut for the camera tripods....

Lastly, there is an inscription of an ostrich... As you walk along the ledge just before your enter the canyon to your upper left you will see a flat surface of rock. Here you can see the inscription of an ostrich, a testament of time and the different wildlife that was once in the Wadi Rum desert...

28. Purchase the children's e-book "Bedouin Bedtime", also by Um A'yube

I wrote and illustrated this little book for young children as a way of sharing a little glimpse into Bedouin culture and lifestyle with the world.

The modern world is fast paced, demanding, complicated. Bedouin life offers an antidote to the modern world, slowing us down, grounding us in nature. This message I would like to share with children through my work, and I would like to use the work as a way to preserve Bedouin lifestyle, and to share diversity. Fear often comes from the unknown and when children are exposed to cultures from all over the world through travel and other mediums like the books they grow up with, then they develop open fearless minds.

This little e-book is great for families with young children who are travelling. No-one wants to take a bag of books with them on holiday so an e-book is a good solution to enable reading to continue while on a journey (not to mention the trees you save as well). The short story is ideal for toddlers or as an early reader for older children who are just getting started reading.

The simple sentences and bold illustrations take the reader on a starry journey through the bedtime routine of Bedouin nomads.

This little e-book is an ideal companion for your children on their trip to Wadi Rum.

29. Ride a camel through the desert

Camels are extraordinary animals, and without them it is doubtful Bedouin people would have survived their nomadic life in the desert. This relationship is still an important one for Bedouin people and most people will keep at least one camel if they are financially able. Camels are used for tourism and as milk camels. Camel milk is very nutritious and if you were to get lost in the desert with your milk camel (na-ger) you could survive on her milk alone, for around 6 months. Each camel has a distinct character, you can get quiet ones and feisty ones. Regardless of the character all males become very difficult when the she-camels are in season in the winter. At this time of year the loud angry sounding call of the male camels can be heard echoing through the village with much more frequency than normal. Female camels are pregnant for one year and then the baby camel will nurse for around 1 year.

Riding a camel is usually very uncomfortable and a good way to experience directly the reality of Bedouin nomadic life (hard). If you are flexible you may not find it too uncomfortable. Even if you are not ready for a full day or multiple day trek I think it is worthwhile even if for one hour, just to experience the desert from a different perspective.

One lady once said to me upon mounting her camel for the first time "Wow I feel in scale up here!"

Fun Fact: When you see a camels walking together in single file they have a plan to go for a long way.

30. Wake up for sunrise

You may see the sunrise as a part of getting up to go to work, or you may even be a Muslim and get up before sunrise to pray. However, even if you have enjoyed many sunrises you have not ever seen one in the desert of Wadi Rum. The light show as the sun gradually arrives and the blacks, grays, blues of the night make way to reveal the multitude of colours in the mountains, sand and sky, is something every visitor to Wadi Rum should experience. You don't need a special tour, or even to be at a camp with a view to the sunrise. Just set your alarm and go for a short early morning walk before breakfast. The true beauty of watching the sunrise actually comes when you look to the West. The West is where the magic happens. As the light emerges from the East, the desert is transformed. Slowly the colours of the landscape are revealed, like a veil being lifted by the wind.

>TOURIST – Wadi Rum, Jordan – Um A'yube

There is a quality about the desert that is unlike anything else I have encountered. It creates the sensation of being utterly alone, with an extension of physical distance beyond which is the unlimited extension of time itself. In this environment, the human mind is lifted out of itself, above the level of mundane existence, until one has the feeling of being cast out into a limitless world of endless space and time.

— **Edward Nevins and Theon Wright, World without Time, The Bedouin**

>TOURIST – Wadi Rum, Jordan – Um A'yube

31. Scramble up one of the many small mountains to watch the sunset

Watching the sunset is another special time in the desert of Wadi Rum. As the sun sinks the light softens and you will find a multitude of colours explode and reward you with a wonderful show. For me the most special thing about the sunset is not the moment the sun sinks but the hours approaching that time when the shadows lengthen and the beauty of the desert really shines. These "golden hours" are the best time for photography. Scrambling up one of the small little knarly mountains you find all around the desert gives you the best panoramas and an opportunity to capture the beauty with your camera.

32. Visit the "heart" of Wadi Rum

An unassuming rock in the area of desert between the Visitor Center and Rum Village is known locally as the as the "heart of Wadi Rum". You could easily walk to the rock from the road independently, or ask your guide to include it in your tour. The views are lovely from the rock looking down the valley to Rum village, set in a sandy open plain, between the towering mountains either side of the valley. This is where the Arab army of the great Arab revolt traveled down from the North to South. Stopping at Al-Shillellah Spring to water and meet with the local Sheikh's. In the book the "Seven Pillars of Wisdom", Lawrence of Arabia describes the army travelling down this valley and being dwarfed by the scale of it. Viewing the valley from the "heart" of Wadi Rum gives a good perspective, better than the perspective you get from the road.

Google maps: 29.624412, 35.436170

GPS: 29°37'27.9"N 35°26'10.2"E

33. Watch Bedouin coffee being prepared and have a taste

Bedouin coffee is more than just coffee. Bedouin coffee is a ritual and an art form. First the green coffee beans are roasted over the fire using an large metal plate with a long handle, and a long handled metal spatula. The coffee is lightly roasted constantly being turned with the spatula. Once the coffee is roasted it is pounded in a large brass pestle. As the coffee is pounded the mortar is struck against the side and the ringing sound produced used to be a "summons" or an open invitation to passing Bedouin to come and visit for coffee. The coffee is then removed from the pestle and cardamom is pounded. In the meantime water is brought to the boil over the fire in a special tall coffee pot, with a long high spout. Once the water is boiling the coffee is added, and allowed to turn over a little in the boiling water, the cardamom is added, turns a little in the boiling water then the pot is removed from the heat. The result is a light in colour, rich, fragrant coffee that even I, a non coffee drinker likes. Coffee is not usually provided for tourists at the camps because of the effort and time involved, also because of the cost.

However, you may find people will be happy to offer the service on request so you can experience Bedouin coffee.

Coffee is always provided at weddings, funerals, and when people visit after the birth of a child. Coffee is also drunk after the evening meal during Ramadan and when people "azoom nas" (call people) – invite them around for a meal. Coffee is drunk in small wide brimmed cups, usually quickly in one go.

There is symbolism when drinking coffee. One cup as a guest, the second as friends, the third you indicate your unshakable loyalty/ affiliation to the family/ tribe you are visiting. Coffee cups are never placed on the ground but returned directly to the person taking the coffee around to the guests. When you don't want more you shake the cup as you return it to the person serving you.

34. Spend at least one day at your Bedouin camp in the desert, with no activities planned

The desert of Wadi Rum is particularly extraordinary when you are alone. The silence you feel when there is no one around, no Jeep, no camels, no wind, is like nothing you will experience anywhere else. The silence is oppressive, heavy, you find yourself straining your ears, you feel grateful then for the sound of the wind, any wind that might breeze by. Alone in the desert you are face to face with yourself, and spending time alone is a wonderful way to practice mindfulness, to reflect on your life, or even to find God.

Most Bedouin camps will allow you to spend time at the camp and not arrange any activities.

Make sure you take water with you when walking independently around, also make multiple short hikes rather than one long one. This will help you get orientated in the area and not get lost.

35. Taste some fresh dates (khalal or rutab)

During the harvest season you can find fresh dates on sale, the khalal dates are fresh from the tree, yellow, crunchy, sweet and delicious.

The rutab dates, my personal favorite, are available all year around. They are fully ripened, but still very soft, very sweet, and very tasty. I have never seen dates like this available in the UK, so I think while you are in the Middle East you must take the opportunity to try them.

Both kinds can be found in the village, the khalal dates are only available in the autumn during the date harvest. The rutab dates can be found in the village shops. The best kind is packaged in a rectangular cardboard box – white with red, green and brown writing and images on them.

36. Play with some Bedouin children

Bedouin children are mischievous, fun, creative, resourceful, strong, and hilarious. The best way to gain insight into any culture is by spending time with children. They will react when you do something strange, even point it out and you will see them as their unrestrained selves.

Children are always happy for small gifts but I don't encourage giving them money as this can then prompt them to ask tourists walking though the village when they see them. If you do like to give money then small change like 5 or 10 fils is plenty. If you like to bring little gifts for children then things like bubbles, balloons, pens/ pencils, nice paper/ book will always go down well...

37. Visit a secret winding sand dune "canyon"

Most tours drive right past this place, and perhaps it is a good thing as the feature is therefore, somewhat protected. This is one of my favorite places not too far from the village. Potentially you could walk there independently if you have GPS.

As you walk North, up the valley parallel to the Wadi Rum valley (East side), with a block of mountains in between that includes Jebel Ishrin, you approach what looks like a single tall sand dune. Then as you get closer you realise that there are two sand dunes running parallel to each other in a winding curve. The result is a short winding canyon with a tall sand dune for the walls either side. This is a unique and special place to visit. As a bonus if you climb to the top of one of the dunes you get really lovely views South to Jebel Khazali. The place is ideal for a picnic or for a night of Bivouac camping.

Google map co-ordinates: 29.560955, 35.446035

GPS: 29°33'39.4"N 35°26'45.7"E.

38. Prepare some riddles and jokes to tell around the fire

Most evenings in Wadi Rum will at some point finish sitting around a fire, enjoying the warmth and good company of your guide and other guests. Bedouin people love jokes and riddles, and for sure you will be told at least a few during your visit to Wadi Rum. Why not have some of your own ready as well, this will help the evening be a social one of mutual exchange.

39. Listen to Bedouin music – Bedouin singing and Oud playing

There is something very special about unplugged Bedouin music. Rustic, gravelly, hauntingly beautiful, rhythmic. The music is very much a reflection of the desert itself. Originally many, many years ago Bedouin people would just sing and clap without any kind of instruments. They use the singing to tell long stories about their tribe, and/or historical events. Then later in time they gained access to the Oud and began to use this instrument as well. The music is very earthy and the rhythms remind me of the rhythm of a camel. Most camps will play some music as a free "bonus" in the evenings. They may not do this every night so if you are keen to hear someone play then you should mention it when booking. Not necessarily every camp has a musician in the team and they may need to call someone specially to come that night. Most musicians are self taught and they learn just by watching and listening to others play, and then copying the methods themselves.

40. Visit during a full moon

One of my tips is to come to Wadi Rum when the moon is small. However, if you cannot, then visiting during a full moon is also a wonderful experience. The moon lights up the desert at night with a silvery light, and allows night walks without need of a torch/ flashlight. The full moon transforms the desert into a mythical and mysterious place...

>TOURIST – Wadi Rum, Jordan – Um A'yube

For this was the real desert where differences of race and colour, of wealth and social standing, are almost meaningless; where coverings of pretence are stripped away and basic truths emerge.
— **Wilfred Thesiger, Arabian Sands**

41. Take a walk around Rum village

Rum Village is a small village of about 2-3,000 people. There is a girl's school on the East side of the village, and a boys school on the West side of the village. There is a Masjid (mosque) on the West side. There are various small village shops providing food for the village and for the guides operating their Bedouin camps in the desert. You will see a varying degree of development. Some houses are well built, and some are more modest, according to the means of the families to which they belong. You will often see black goat hair tents next to or outside the houses, this is because most Bedouin people still feel most at home in a tent. You will see people still keep goats, sheep, camels, chickens, pigeons and a few families have geese. You may also spot some domesticated rabbits. People keep the rabbits for food and sometimes they escape and can be seen hopping around. There is a health clinic which also has an ambulance. The village is mostly made up of Bedouin people from a variety of tribes – the majority being Zalabieh and Zaweidah, but there are other tribes in smaller numbers too. There are also some Egyptian people, Sudanese people (they have been here around 10-15 yrs), and now more recently some Syrian people are making their way to the area. There are also a few Westerners who make Wadi Rum their home..

42. Follow tracks in the sand

While on your tour you will see a multitude of different tracks winding through the sand. Usually you can see lizard, camel, bird, beetle, dog, goat and gerbil tracks. You may see ant roads too. If you are lucky you may spot wild rabbit, fox, hedgehog, hydrax, or even snake tracks. You can read little dramas that have taken place, where perhaps a lizard has been running away from a bird, or a gerbil has been busy collecting food in the night.

43. Count shooting stars

No visit to Wadi Rum is replete without a walk under the stars or full moon. If you are walking under the stars take a blanket with you and take the time to relax in comfort, look up and see how many shooting stars you can count. You are highly likely to be amazed as shooting stars are regularly seen. You can even look up on the internet when there are meteorite showers due, to time your visit for a particularly spectacular show. In winter make sure to wrap up warm when you walk in the night. Take your flashlight, don't go too far from your camp and pay attention to the route you take... It can be easy to get lost in the night as everything looks very different.

.

44. Try to spot a desert hedgehog

Desert hedgehogs are very common in Wad Rum. At most camps if you sit quietly in the early evening not too far from the kitchen or bathroom you have a good chance to see one. Usually camps have regular hedgehog visitors. They come for the water and chicken bones... Bedouin people like hedgehogs very much because they will eat snakes and scorpions. The best time of year to see them is the summer, autumn and spring. They are less active in the winter.

45. Don't forget to look down

Wadi Rum is a desert of majestic views, sweeping vistas, soaring contrasts, panoramic wonders. When you visit your eyes will be met by an onslaught of dramatic landscapes. However, please don't forget to look down. There are some fascinating features under your nose (or your toes), and if you look down you will have the opportunity to appreciate the macro Wadi Rum too. You will notice the different types of sand, the textures, colours, how they blend and meet each other. You will notice the diverse range of stones and the tiny lives of the insects that eek out their lives in the desert. You will notice the flora of the desert, often flowers are miniature in their bid to survive, tiny bursts of life hidden in little rock cracks, or precariously clinging onto a ledge.

Look around but don't forget to look down too.

46. Take a silly action selfie jumping over a sand dune

My favorite sand dune for silly sand dune jumping photographs is the small red one close to the Um Sabbatah Mountain.

Google maps: 29.463432, 35.407287

GPS: 29°27'48.4"N 35°24'26.2"E

Um Sabbatah sand dune is also an excellent spot for seeing the sunset from. This sand dune is by far the best sand dune for running and jumping action shots. The dune is not very high but on the West side there is a kind of "drop" which is great fun to run and jump off. Have a blast trying to capture your antics in a photo... it is not as easy as it looks.

>TOURIST – Wadi Rum, Jordan – Um A'yube

47. Watch your Bedouin guide change a flat tyre

Bedouin people are very practical and skilled people. Living in the desert makes most tasks difficult. The difficulty of the desert gives Bedouin people training from a young age in many skills we have pretty much lost in the west. Such as making a fire, climbing mountains, managing/taking care of animals, milking a goat or camel and many other practical things we don't have a clue about. A lot of young boys will be driving or at least learning by 12 yrs (in the desert not on the main roads). Along with driving they will know how to fix a Jeep and most importantly change a tyre. Most of the time Bedouin people will not own a jack so they have a method to change the tyre using stones instead. If you get a puncture while on your tour, don't worry, sit back and be amazed.

48. Learn about Bedouin herb/ plant use

Bedouin people collect herbs and plants from the desert, and use the flora for medicinal and other uses (there is one which is used as soap). Some plants are edible too... some are salty and can be added to a salad in small amounts, another one is like a small parsnip/carrot and is called "old ladies legs". Most Bedouin guides will know about these plants just let them know it interests you and they will usually point them out when they see them.

The absolute best time to come to Wadi Rum if you are interested in the flora of the desert is March and April. If we have had a good year for rain you will see carpets of miniature purple, yellow and white flowers everywhere. At this time of year you will find anyone who owns goats and camels will be in the desert grazing their animals as much as they can. This ensures the animals grow fat and tasty, and the burden of buying food for the flock is lessened.

49. See how many different types of rock you can count

The rocks in Wadi Rum are extremely diverse. There is sandstone which comes in various colours and textures, the most predominant colours are red and white/yellow. Then you have granite. This is usually found at the base of mountains as a rock layer under the sandstone layers, mostly I see pink granite but there are other colours too. There are slates in purple grey shades, reds. You can also find hard black basalt – my favourite. There are smooth round pebbles in white, red, grey they look like they were shaped by water, at the bottom of a river or lake. They can often be found in seams in the sandstone mountains. You can find flints, rocks with copper in and other kinds of crystals and minerals.

A lot of interesting information about the protected area, the geography, history, and the wildlife can be found on the UNESCO world heritage site: http://whc.unesco.org/en/list/1377/

Lichen also grows in the desert of Wadi Rum; mostly you will find it in nooks and crannies where there is the least amount of sun, growing on the rock faces. You can also find fossilised lichen on some rocks.

There are also small hard bleached white snail shells to find which are pretty cool to me! I saw a live snail for the first time only this year...

Rocks, shells, plants and sand should not be removed from the protected area. Please satisfy yourself with taking pictures and being a responsible tourist.

50. Disconnect yourself from the world (just keep your camera with you)

Wadi Rum is first of all a beautiful desert environment, a natural landscape. The desert is vast, huge and you are dwarfed in its presence. Visiting this beautiful place on earth is a perfect opportunity to take some time to escape from modern life. Visiting Wadi Rum gives you time to escape from the hustle, bustle, rush, drive, and competition of the West. Most camps will not have reception so disconnect, relax and enjoy reality, the present, the moment …

>TOURIST – Wadi Rum, Jordan – Um A'yube

> TOURIST

Please read other Greater than a Tourist Books.

Join the >Tourist Mailing List :
http://eepurl.com/cxspyf

Facebook:
https://www.facebook.com/GreaterThanATourist

Pinterest:
http://pinterest.com/GreaterThanATourist

Instagram:
http://Instagram.com/GreaterThanATourist

> TOURIST

Greater than a Tourist

Please leave your honest review of this book on Amazon and Goodreads. Thank you.

>TOURIST

Greater than a Tourist

You can find Greater Than a Tourist books on Amazon.